Slithering Snakes

RATTLESNAKES

GAIL TERP

BLACK RABBIT BOOKS

Bolt is published by Black Rabbit Books
P.O. Box 3263, Mankato, Minnesota, 56002.
www.blackrabbitbooks.com
Copyright © 2021 Black Rabbit Books

Marysa Storm, editor; Grant Gould, designer;
Omay Ayres, photo researcher

Names: Terp, Gail, 1951- author.
Title: Rattlesnakes / by Gail Terp.
Description: Mankato, Minnesota : Black Rabbit Books, [2021] | Series:
Bolt. slithering snakes | Includes bibliographical references and index.
Audience: Ages 8-12 | Audience: Grades 4-6 | Summary: "Diagrams,
graphs, and fun text help readers explore the habitats, diets, and daily
lives of rattlesnakes"– Provided by publisher.
Identifiers: LCCN 2019026727 (print) | LCCN 2019026728 (ebook) |
ISBN 9781623102753 (hardcover) | ISBN 9781644663714 (paperback) |
ISBN 9781623103699 (ebook)
Subjects: LCSH: Rattlesnakes–Juvenile literature.
Classification: LCC QL666.O69 T475 2021 (print) | LCC QL666.O69 (ebook) |
DDC 597.96/38–dc23
LC record available at https://lccn.loc.gov/2019026727
LC ebook record available at https://lccn.loc.gov/2019026728

Special thanks to Jessica McCarthy for her help with this book.

Printed in the United States. 2/20

Image Credits
Alamy: Jeff Lepore, 21 (main); John
Cancalosi, 18; Robert Eastman, 24 (bob-
cat); AnimalsAnimals: Michael Francis, Cover;
Dreamstime: Rusty Dodson, 15 (top); iStock: Tee-
roy, 1; Minden Pictures: Daniel Heuclin, 10–11; David
Welling, 12; John Cancalosi, 22; Kim Taylor, 28; Lynn M.
Stone, 6; MYN / JP Lawrence, 24 (lizard); MYN / Seth Patter-
son, 31; Michael D. Kern, 32; Pete Oxford, 22–23; mwcboard.
com: Old_SD_Dude, 14; Science Source: John Mitchell, 4–5;
Shutterstock: blackboard1965, 16–17; CLS Digital Arts, 24
(rabbit); Eric Isselee, 16, 21 (silhouettes), 24 (rattlesnakes);
fivespots, 24 (snake); Joe McDonald, 27; Le Do, 24 (hawk);
Matt Jeppson, 15 (btm); Rusty Dodson, 8–9; Tim Zurowski,
24 (bird); xradiophotog, 3
Every effort has been made to contact copyright
holders for material reproduced in this book.
Any omissions will be rectified in subsequent
printings if notice is given to
the publisher.

BOLT

CONTENTS

CHAPTER 1

Rattlesnakes in ACTION

A hungry rattlesnake flicks its forked tongue. The tongue will catch the scent of nearby **prey**. The snake's heat sensors are active too. If an animal comes close, the snake will feel its heat.

Something is coming. It's a mouse. The rattlesnake coils into position. Then it strikes. Its fangs push **venom** into the prey. Once the mouse is dead, the snake swallows it whole.

eastern diamondback rattlesnake

timber rattlesnake

COMPARING LENGTHS

black-tailed rattlesnake

pygmy rattlesnake

feet   1

Blending In

There are more than 30 types of rattlesnakes. They're all powerful, venomous **predators**. These snakes have triangle-shaped heads and heavy bodies. They come in several colors. Some are brown, gray, or yellow. Their skin is often marked with patterns. Their colors and patterns help them blend in with their habitats.

3 to 8 feet (1 to 2.4 meters)

3 to 5 feet (1 to 1.5 m)

2 to 4 feet (.6 to 1.2 m)

1 to 2 feet (.3 to .6 m)

2   3   4   5   6   7   8

Listen!

A rattlesnake's tail ends with a rattle. The rattle is made up of rings. When the snake senses a predator, it shakes its tail. This action causes the rings to clink together, making a rattling noise. The noise acts as a warning. Often, the source of danger backs away. If it doesn't, the snake attacks.

Rattlesnakes strike faster than a person can blink.

RATTLESNAKE FEATURES

EYES

RATTLE

FORKED TONGUE

HEAT-SENSING PITS

PATTERNED SKIN

Rattlesnakes are dangerous even with their heads chopped off. Their heads can still bite for a few hours after death!

CHAPTER 2

HUNTING and Homes

Rattlesnakes eat small **mammals**, such as mice. They eat birds and lizards too. These snakes often hide and wait for prey. Once prey comes near, they attack.

Habitats

These snakes are found in North and South America. They live in deserts and grasslands. They also live on rocky hills and mountains. Some even slither through swamps. Rattlesnakes live where there are plenty of hiding places. They need to stay hidden from prey. They must hide from predators too.

Rattlesnakes are good swimmers.

GRASSLANDS

DESERTS

Rattlesnake Range Map

Some rattlesnakes share their **dens** with other types of snakes.

CHAPTER 3

FAMILY Life

Rattlesnakes spend most of their time alone. But many gather in dens for the cold part of the year. In dens, they **brumate** and keep each other warm.

Rattlesnakes also meet up to **mate**. Males find females by following their scent trails. After mating, females give birth. Unlike some other snakes, rattlesnakes don't lay eggs. Instead, the eggs develop inside the females. They then give birth to live young.

No Rattle Yet

Newborn rattlesnakes don't have rattles. But in about two weeks, babies **shed** their skin for the first time. That's when the rattlesnakes get their first rings. Each time the snakes shed, their rattles get another ring. Soon, it's time to make some noise!

Prey should beware of the babies from the start, though. Newborns have fangs and venom. They're ready to catch and kill prey.

COMPARING SIZES

| ADULT EASTERN DIAMONDBACK RATTLESNAKE | NEWBORN EASTERN DIAMONDBACK RATTLESNAKE |

3 to 8 FEET
(1 to 2.4 m)

1 to 1.25 FEET
(.3 m)

BY THE NUMBERS

UP TO 20
number of young that mothers have at one time

8.2 FEET (2.5 M)
LONGEST RECORDED RATTLESNAKE
(EASTERN DIAMONDBACK)

up to 10 pounds
(5 kilograms)
HOW MUCH EASTERN
DIAMONDBACKS WEIGH

10 to 25 years

LIFE SPAN
(all kinds)

Rattlesnake Food Chain

This food chain shows what eats rattlesnakes.
It also shows what rattlesnakes eat.

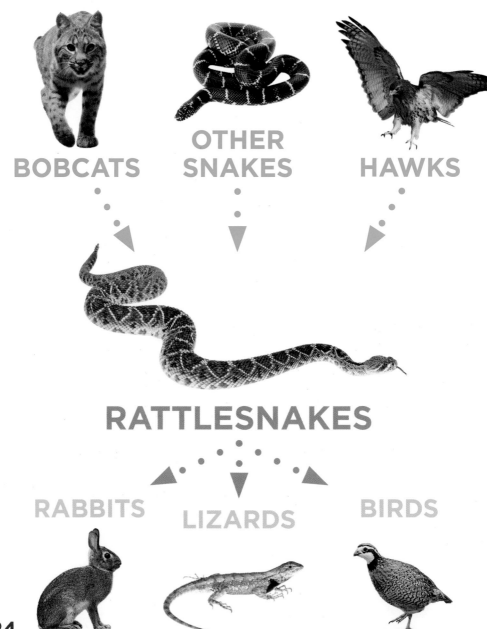

BOBCATS OTHER SNAKES HAWKS

RATTLESNAKES

RABBITS LIZARDS BIRDS

CHAPTER 4

Part of THEIR WORLD

Rattlesnakes are dangerous. But they still have predators. Large birds, such as hawks, eat them. Bobcats and other mammals eat them too. Even other snakes eat them!

Humans also cause problems for rattlesnakes. They hunt the snakes for food and their skin. People turn the skin into wallets and boots. Humans are also destroying the snakes' habitats.

Helpful Rattlesnakes

Some people kill rattlesnakes because they fear them. They worry the snakes will bite them or their pets. In some states, groups of people gather to kill the snakes.

Rattlesnakes might be scary, but they help humans. Rattlesnakes eat mice and other pests. They keep pest populations down. Rattlesnake venom is used in research too. Scientists think it could be used to make medicine.

Protecting Rattlesnakes

Some types of rattlesnakes are **endangered**. Without care, they might die out. Rattlesnakes play a key role in their habitats. They are food for some animals. They keep other animal populations in control. It's important for people to protect rattlesnakes.

Some rattlesnakes are protected in certain U.S. states. It's against the law to kill them.

GLOSSARY

brumate (BREW-mayt)—to spend the winter resting or not moving

den (DEN)—the home of some kinds of wild animals

endangered (in-DAYN-jurd)—close to becoming extinct

mammal (MAH-muhl)—a type of animal that feeds milk to its young and usually has hair or fur

mate (MAYT)—to join together to produce young

predator (PRED-uh-tuhr)—an animal that eats other animals

prey (PRAY)—an animal hunted or killed for food

shed (SHED)—to lose or cast aside a natural covering or part

venom (VEH-num)—a poison made by animals used to kill or injure

BOOKS

Bankston, John. *Rattlesnakes*. All about Snakes. Hallandale, FL: Mitchell Lane Publishers, 2019.

Rathburn, Betsy. *Diamondback Rattlesnakes*. North American Animals. Minneapolis: Bellwether Media, Inc., 2018.

Sprott, Gary. *Western Diamondback Rattlesnake*. World's Coolest Snakes. North Mankato, MN: Rourke Educational Media, 2019.

WEBSITES

Eastern Diamondback Rattlesnake for Kids
**www.ducksters.com/animals/
diamondbackrattler.php**

Rattlesnake
animals.sandiegozoo.org/animals/rattlesnake

Rattlesnake
**kids.nationalgeographic.com/animals/
rattlesnake/#rattlesnake-tongue.jpg**

INDEX